D0581560

To: ....................................................

From: ....................................................

# POSITIVELY
## POOH

*A Coffee Companion
for Any Time of Day*

# EGMONT

*We bring stories to life*

First published in Great Britain 2006 by Egmont UK Limited
239 Kensington High Street, London W8 6SA

Selected text from *WINNIE-THE-POOH* and *THE HOUSE AT POOH CORNER* by A. A. Milne
© The Trustees of the Pooh Properties

Line drawings © E.H. Shepard, colouring © 1970, 1973 and 1974 E.H. Shepard and Egmont UK Ltd

Sketches from THE POOH SKETCHBOOK copyright © 1982 Lloyds TSB Bank PLC
Executors of the Estate of E.H. Shepard, and the E.H. Shepard Trust

This edition © 2006 The Trustees of the Pooh Properties

Book design and new text © 2006 Egmont UK Ltd
Text by Emily Stead and Janette Marshall

ISBN 1 4052 2385 5
ISBN 978 1 4052 2385 0

3 5 7 9 10 8 6 4 2

Printed and bound in Malaysia

# POSITIVELY
# POOH

## A Coffee Companion
## for Any Time of Day

A.A. Milne
Illustrated by E.H. Shepard

**EGMONT**

# A buzz at breakfast will boost your whole day

'When you wake up in the morning,
Pooh,' said Piglet at last,
'what's the first thing you say to yourself?'
'What's for breakfast?' said Pooh.
'What do *you* say, Piglet?'
'I say, I wonder what's going to happen
exciting *to-day*?' said Piglet.
Pooh nodded thoughtfully.
'It's the same thing,' he said.

# A little something
## can go a long way

Pooh always liked a little something at eleven o'clock in the morning, and he was very glad to see Rabbit getting out the plates and mugs; and when Rabbit said, 'Honey or condensed milk with your bread?' he was so excited that he said, 'Both,' and then, so as not to seem greedy, he added, 'But don't bother about the bread, please.' And for a long time after that he said nothing . . . until at last, humming to himself in a rather sticky voice, he got up, shook Rabbit lovingly by the paw, and said that he must be going on.

# Are you sitting comfortably?

[Eeyore] looked round at them in his
melancholy way. 'I suppose none of you are
sitting on a thistle by any chance?'
'I believe I am,' said Pooh. 'Ow!' He got up, and
looked behind him. 'Yes, I was. I thought so.'
'Thank you, Pooh. If you've quite finished with it.'
He moved across to Pooh's place, and began to eat.

They began to talk in a friendly way
about this and that, and Piglet said,
'If you see what I mean, Pooh,' and
Pooh said, 'It's just what I think myself,
Piglet,' and Piglet said, 'But, on the
other hand, Pooh, we must remember,'
and Pooh said, 'Quite true, Piglet,
although I had forgotten it for the moment.'

# Find time for friendly conversations

# Keep good Company

Well, [Pooh] was humming this hum to himself,
and walking gaily along, wondering what everybody
else was doing, and what it felt like, being
somebody else, when suddenly he came to a
sandy bank, and in the bank was a large hole.
'Aha!' said Pooh. (*Rum-tum-tiddle-um-tum.*) 'If I know
anything about anything, that hole means Rabbit,'
he said, 'and Rabbit means Company,' he said, 'and
Company means Food and Listening-to-Me-Humming
and such like. *Rum-tum-tum-tiddle-um.*'

'No Give and Take,' Eeyore went on . . .
'It's your fault, Eeyore. You've never been to see
any of us. You just stay here in this one corner of
the Forest waiting for the others to come to you.
Why don't you go to them sometimes?'
Eeyore was silent for a little while, thinking.
'There may be something in what you say, Rabbit,'
he said at last. 'I have been neglecting you.
I must move about more. I must come and go.'
'That's right, Eeyore. Drop in on any of us at
any time, when you feel like it.'

Drop in on neighbours
(you can always
drop out again)

# Feeling eleven o'clockish?

'Shall I look, too?' said Pooh,
who was beginning to feel a
little eleven o'clockish.
And he found a small tin of
condensed milk, and something
seemed to tell him that Tiggers
didn't like this, so he took it
into a corner by itself, and went
with it to see that nobody
interrupted it.

Suddenly Christopher Robin began to laugh . . .
and he laughed . . . and he laughed . . .
and he laughed . . .
'Oh, Bear!' said Christopher Robin. 'How I do love you!'
'So do I,' said Pooh.

# We love those who make us laugh

Swap de-caf for de-stress...
daydream!

Piglet was sitting on the ground at the door of his house blowing happily at a dandelion, and wondering whether it would be this year, next year, sometime, or never. He had just discovered that it would be never, and was trying to remember what '*it*' was, and hoping it wasn't anything nice, when Pooh came up.

A kind word
costs nothing

'I see now,' said Winnie-the-Pooh.
'I have been Foolish and Deluded,' said he,
'and I am a Bear of No Brain at All.'
'You're the Best Bear in All the World,'
said Christopher Robin soothingly.
'Am I?' said Pooh hopefully. And then he
brightened up suddenly.
'Anyhow,' he said, 'it is nearly Luncheon Time.'
So he went home for it.

# We all need someone to lean on

'Good morning, Christopher Robin,' [Pooh] called out.
'Hallo, Pooh Bear. I can't get this boot on.'
'That's bad,' said Pooh.
'Do you think you could very kindly lean against me,
'cos I keep pulling so hard that I fall over backwards.'
Pooh sat down, dug his feet into the ground,
and pushed hard against Christopher Robin's back,
and Christopher Robin pushed hard against his,
and pulled and pulled at his boot until he had got it on.
'And that's that,' said Pooh.
'Thank you, Pooh.'

# Do Nothing: it's good for you

'What I like *doing* best is Nothing.'
'How do you do Nothing?' asked Pooh,
after he had wondered for a long time.
'Well, it's when people call out at you just as
you're going off to do it, "What are you going to do,
Christopher Robin?" and you say "Oh, nothing,"
and then you go and do it.'
'Oh, I see,' said Pooh.
'This is a nothing sort of thing that we're doing now.'
'Oh, I see,' said Pooh again.
'It means just going along, listening to all the
things you can't hear, and not bothering.'
'Oh!' said Pooh.

*Sing Ho! for the life of a Bear!*
*Sing Ho! for the life of a Bear!*
*I don't much mind if it rains or snows,*
*'Cos I've got a lot of honey on my nice new nose!*
*I don't much care if it snows or thaws,*
*'Cos I've got a lot of honey on my nice clean paws!*
*Sing Ho! for a Bear!*
*Sing Ho! for a Pooh!*
*And I'll have a little something in an hour or two!*

# Life is good, so Sing Ho!

# Maintain some youthful enthusiasm

By the time it came to the edge of the Forest the stream had grown up, so that it was almost a river, and, being grown-up, it did not run and jump and sparkle along as it used to do when it was younger, but moved more slowly. For it knew now where it was going, and it said to itself, 'There is no hurry. We shall get there some day.' But all the little streams higher up in the Forest went this way and that, quickly, eagerly, having so much to find out before it was too late.

Can't find what you're looking for?

# Try Pooh's logic . . .

'How would it be?' said Pooh slowly, 'if, as soon as we're out of sight of this Pit, we try to find it again?'

'What's the good of that?' said Rabbit.

'Well,' said Pooh, 'we keep looking for Home and not finding it, so I thought that if we looked for this Pit, we'd be sure not to find it, which would be a Good Thing, because then we might find something that we *weren't* looking for, which might be just what we *were* looking for, really.'

'A week!' said Pooh gloomily. '*What about meals?*'
'I'm afraid no meals,' said Christopher Robin,
'because of getting thin quicker.
But we *will* read to you.'
Bear began to sigh, and then found he
couldn't because he was so tightly stuck;
and a tear rolled down his eye, as he said:
'Then would you read a Sustaining Book,
such as would help and comfort a
Wedged Bear in Great Tightness?'
So for a week Christopher Robin read that
sort of book at the North end of Pooh,
and Rabbit hung his washing on the South end.

Make the most of
time stuck indoors

# Try meditating –
# if a donkey can do it . . .

The Old Grey Donkey, Eeyore, stood by himself in a thistly corner of the Forest, his front feet well apart, his head on one side, and thought about things. Sometimes he thought sadly to himself, 'Why?' and sometimes he thought, 'Wherefore?' and sometimes he thought, 'Inasmuch as which?' – and sometimes he didn't quite know what he *was* thinking about.

# A Bear with Brain listens to his body!

[Pooh] hadn't gone more than half-way when a
sort of funny feeling began to creep all over him.
It began at the tip of his nose and trickled all
through him and out at the soles of his feet.
It was just as if somebody inside him were saying,
'Now then, Pooh, time for a little something.'

'Dear, dear,' said Pooh, 'I didn't
know it was as late as that.'
So he sat down and took the
top off his jar of honey.
'Lucky I brought this
with me,' he thought.

'Many a bear going out on
a warm day like this
would never have thought
of bringing a little
something with him.'
And he began to eat.

Good friends are always
pleased to see you

'Pooh!' squeaked the voice.

'It's Piglet!' cried Pooh eagerly.

'Where are you?'

'Underneath,' said Piglet in an underneath sort of way.

'Underneath what?'

'You,' squeaked Piglet. 'Get up!'

'Oh!' said Pooh, and scrambled up as quickly as he could.

'Did I fall on you, Piglet?'

'You fell on me,' said Piglet, feeling himself all over.

'I didn't mean to,' said Pooh sorrowfully.

'I didn't mean to be underneath,'

said Piglet sadly. 'But I'm all right now,

Pooh, and I *am* so glad it was you.'

# Indulge in some do-not-disturb time

'Is anybody at home?'
There was a sudden scuffling noise from
inside the hole, and then silence.
'What I said was, "Is anybody at home?"'
called out Pooh very loudly.
'No!' said a voice; and then added,
'You needn't shout so loud. I heard you
quite well the first time.'
'Bother!' said Pooh. 'Isn't there anybody here at all?'
'Nobody.'

Big or small,
be kind to all

Kanga said very kindly, 'Well, look in my cupboard, Tigger dear, and see what you'd like.'
Because she knew at once that, however big Tigger seemed to be, he wanted as much kindness as Roo.

Everyone needs a
Thoughtful Spot

Half-way between Pooh's house and Piglet's
house was a Thoughtful Spot where they met
sometimes when they had decided to go and see
each other, and as it was warm and out of the wind
they would sit down there for a little and wonder what
they would do now that they *had* seen each other.

# Bees and trees will calm and soothe

One day Rabbit and Piglet were sitting outside Pooh's front door listening to Rabbit, and Pooh was sitting with them. It was a drowsy summer afternoon, and the Forest was full of gentle sounds, which all seemed to be saying to Pooh, 'Don't listen to Rabbit, listen to me.' So he got into a comfortable position for not listening to Rabbit, and from time to time he opened his eyes to say 'Ah!' and then closed them again . . .

A Very Nearly Tea can
always be squeezed in

Christopher Robin was at home by this time,
because it was the afternoon, and he was so glad to
see them that they stayed there until very nearly
tea-time, and then they had a Very Nearly tea,
which is one you forget about afterwards,
and hurried on to Pooh Corner,
so as to see Eeyore before it
was too late to have a
Proper Tea with Owl.

'The atmospheric conditions have been very unfavourable lately,' said Owl.

'The what?'

'It has been raining,' explained Owl.

'Yes,' said Christopher Robin. 'It has.'

'The flood-level has reached an unprecedented height.'

'The who?'

'There's a lot of water about,' explained Owl.

'Yes,' said Christopher Robin, 'there is.'

'However, the prospects are rapidly becoming more favourable.'

# Start with small talk to brighten up conversations

# Turn an ordinary day into a Friendly Day

'Let's go and see *everybody*,' said Pooh.
'Because when you've been walking in the
wind for miles, and you suddenly go into somebody's
house, and he says, "Hallo, Pooh, you're just in time
for a little smackerel of something," and you are,
then it's what I call a Friendly Day.'

# Discover new treats

Tigger looked up at the ceiling, and closed his eyes,
and his tongue went round and round his chops,
in case he had left any outside, and a peaceful
smile came over his face as he said,
'So *that's* what Tiggers like!'

Stories enrich (as much as smackerels and little somethings)

'Is that the end of the story?' asked Christopher Robin.

'That's the end of that one. There are others.'

'About Pooh and Me?'

'And Piglet and Rabbit and all of you.'

'What are you doing?' [said Pooh.]
'I'm planting a haycorn, Pooh, so that it can
grow up into an oak-tree, and have lots of haycorns
just outside the front door instead of having to
walk miles and miles, do you see, Pooh?'
'Supposing it doesn't?' said Pooh.
'It will, because Christopher Robin says it will,
so that's why I'm planting it.'
'Well,' said Pooh, 'if I plant a honeycomb outside
my house, then it will grow up into a beehive.'
Piglet wasn't quite sure about this.

# Keep your promises

'Pooh, *promise* you won't forget about me, ever.
Not even when I'm a hundred.'
Pooh thought for a little.
'How old shall I be then?'
'Ninety-nine.'
Pooh nodded.
'I promise,' he said.